Movie Monsters

Other Books by Thomas G. Aylesworth

The Alchemists: Magic into Science
Astrology and Foretelling the Future
Into the Mammal's World
It Works Like This
Monsters from the Movies
Mysteries from the Past
Servants of the Devil
Teaching for Thinking
This Vital Air, This Vital Water
Traveling into Tomorrow
Vampires and Other Ghosts
Werewolves and Other Monsters
Who's Out There?

Movie Monsters

THOMAS G. AYLESWORTH

J. B. LIPPINCOTT NEW YORK

This one is for Aaron Klein

American International Pictures, Inc., pages 31, 70; Hammer Film Productions, pages 63, 64, 65, 69 (bottom); Metro-Goldwyn-Mayer, Inc., pages 44, 54; Paramount Pictures, pages 52, 53, 60; RKO (copyrighted-RKO Radio Pictures, a division of RKO General, Inc.), pages 8, 10, 11, 12; Toho International, Inc., pages 14, 16, 17; Twentieth Century-Fox, page 37; Universal Pictures, an MCA, Inc. Company, pages 18, 20, 21, 23, 24, 27, 30, 34, 40, 41, 43, 45, 47, 48, 57, 67 (top), 69 (top).

U.S. Library of Congress Cataloging in Publication Data

Aylesworth, Thomas G
 Movie monsters.

 Filmography: p.
 Includes index.
 SUMMARY: Describes some famous movie monsters, how they were created, and the films in which they appeared.
  1. Horror films—History and criticism—Juvenile literature. [1. Horror films. 2. Monsters] I. Title.
 PN1995.9.H6A94   791.43'7   75-12997
 ISBN 0-397-31639-9
 ISBN 0-397-32467-7 (lib. bdg.)
 ISBN 0-397-31640-2 (pbk.)

Contents

Movie Monsters

Kong surprises the filmmakers. (RKO, 1933)

THE GREATEST APE MONSTER

King Kong

King Kong is a movie about a huge gorilla. He lives on a mysterious island with dinosaurs and other prehistoric animals for neighbors. When some moviemakers come to make a film about the strange animals on the island, Kong falls in love with the woman who is the star of the picture.

So he kidnaps her. Many of the men in the movie crew try to rescue her. Finally, they knock Kong out with a gas bomb and take him to New York City. He escapes and finds the woman. At the end of the picture, he takes her to the top of the Empire State Building. Air Force planes try to shoot him down. Kong, knowing he is dying, puts the woman on the ledge and falls to his death.

No wonder he is killed by the fall. The 102-story Empire State Building was 1,250 feet high in 1933. That's longer than four football fields laid end to

This is what the Empire State Building looked like. And these planes were the pride of the Army Air Corps. (RKO, 1933)

end. The television antenna on top was added later.

There have been other American films about

In *Son of Kong,* the ape was a little smaller than his father. And he was much more gentle. Here he is, protecting two humans. (RKO, 1933)

huge gorillas. You may have seen *Son of Kong* or *Mighty Joe Young.* But Kong was special. He was not like most monsters in movies. Kong did not kill just to be killing. He hurt people only when he was being attacked or when he was trying to protect the woman he loved. At the end of the film, almost everyone in the audience is sorry to see him die.

How were the people in Hollywood able to create an artificial ten-story-tall ape? They didn't. They used a sixteen-inch-high gorilla model. When the model was in position, one frame of the film was exposed. Then the model was moved a tiny bit, and another frame of the film was exposed. And

One of the trick shots from *King Kong.* It has been touched up by an artist. The flying lizard is about to take the girl away, but Kong saves her. (RKO, 1933)

so on. It took ten hours to expose thirty seconds' worth of film.

Also, a huge gorilla hand was built. It was eight feet high. This was for close-up shots. The woman who was the star of the movie could be photographed in this hand.

Whether the moviemakers used the hand or the model, something else was needed. Sometimes they did their photography in front of a backdrop. This might be a motion picture shown behind the model or hand. Or it might be a still photograph. At other times they had to create a model set, such as the Empire State Building scene. Either way, it was shown to a scale that made Kong look huge.

They don't make movies like this anymore in the United States. They can't. The cost is just too high. Imagine paying a whole film crew more than a day's pay to produce only a half minute of film. That runs into a lot of money.

It's the same for war movies with big battle scenes. They aren't made now in this country. It costs too much to hire thousands of men to play the parts of soldiers in the war.

It seems that Japan has taken over the monster pictures. And Italy and Spain have taken over the war films. Wages are lower in those countries.

THE GREATEST REPTILE MONSTER

Godzilla

Godzilla, King of the Monsters, is a movie about a huge reptile. He might be a sort of dinosaur. Or he might be a sort of dragon.

Anyway, being disturbed by an atomic explosion, he comes up out of the Pacific Ocean. He has

Godzilla is about ready to use his atomic breath. (Toho, 1955)

atomic breath and can melt steel with it. He is also big enough to kick over or knock down huge buildings. In the film he destroys the city of Tokyo. But at the end he seems to have been killed by an atomic weapon.

However, he really was not killed, because he came back in other pictures. There was *The Return of Godzilla, Godzilla Versus the Thing,* and *Son of Godzilla.* And even King Kong was brought back for *King Kong Versus Godzilla.* The reason for all these other Godzilla movies was that the first one had been so successful. But in later films he became a hero instead of a villain. Perhaps he was being looked upon as a protector, not a destroyer.

These films were made in Japan. But they were meant to be shown all over the world. You can tell that because the star of *Godzilla, King of the Monsters,* is an American, Raymond Burr. You have probably seen him often in reruns of the TV shows *Perry Mason* and *Ironside.*

With the Godzilla pictures, the Japanese took over where the Americans had left off. Their King Kong was not as realistic as the American model. It looked more like a cheap puppet. But, once again, the pictures were made at less cost in Japan than they could have been made in other countries.

Here is the beginning of a fight in *King Kong Versus Godzilla*. (Toho, 1963)

There is another reason for the fact that Japanese film people turned to movies like this. They were very concerned about the dangers of atomic energy. Remember that they had been attacked with atom bombs during World War II. Japan is the only country in the world to have suffered in that way. The Japanese had seen destroyed cities and diseased people—results of the atomic bombing. Atomic power was more frightening to them than to any other nation.

You might not agree with the choice of Godzilla as the greatest reptile monster. Your favorite reptile might be Rodan, another Japanese dinosaur. He could fly. Or it might be the monster from the

The terrifying Rodan. (Toho, 1957)

The Creature from the Black Lagoon. It was played by Ricou Browning, who later wrote some of the *Flipper* shows. On the right is Julia Adams, wearing the standard white costume. (Universal, 1954)

film *The Creature from the Black Lagoon.* Or it might be the dinosaur from one of the few cowboy-monster movies, *The Beast of Hollow Mountain.*

THE GREATEST MAN-MADE MONSTER
Frankenstein's Creature

The movie *Frankenstein* is the story of a scientist who tries to make an artificial man. The scientist, Dr. Frankenstein, steals spare parts from dead bodies. But his assistant makes a mistake. He steals the brain from a dead criminal.

The body is put together and brought to life. The monster accidentally kills a little girl and causes other problems in the town. Finally, the peasants kill him.

This film was taken from a book, *Frankenstein, or the Modern Prometheus.* It was written by Mary Wollstonecraft Shelley and published in 1818. The story behind the book is most unusual.

Mary Shelley was the wife of a great English poet, Percy Bysshe Shelley. And one of the couple's friends was another famous English poet, Lord Byron. The Shelleys were spending a summer in Switzerland, and Byron was a neighbor.

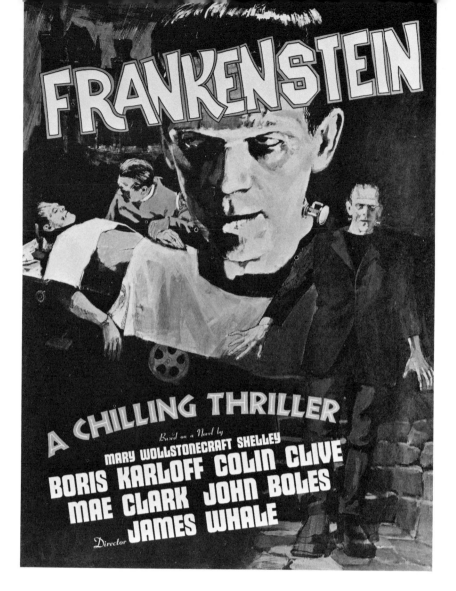

A poster advertising *Frankenstein.* It was printed after the opening of the movie. You can tell this because Boris Karloff's name is listed. The people who made the movie would not tell who played the monster until opening night. Karloff was not even invited to the grand opening. (Universal, 1931)

Here is the scene between the monster and the little girl. She has been throwing flowers into the water. He thinks that beautiful things belong in the water. So he puts the girl in the water and she drowns. It is an accident. The monster doesn't know that people drown. (Universal, 1931)

The summer weather was miserable, and people had to stay indoors. So Byron suggested an amusement. Each of them was to write a ghost story. Byron came up with a tale that became part of his work, *Mazeppa*. Shelley wrote a story about his early life. Another friend, Dr. Polidori, wrote a novel, *The Vampyre*. Mary Shelley's contribution was *Frankenstein*.

The film of *Frankenstein,* made in 1931, was not the first movie based on the book. It wasn't even the second movie about the artificial monster. The first one was made by none other than Thomas A. Edison in 1910. It was a silent picture and starred Charles Ogle. The second one was made in 1915 and was called *Life Without Soul.*

Everyone knows that the 1931 picture starred Boris Karloff. But he was not the first actor to be asked to play the monster. Bela Lugosi was. Lugosi, however, turned down the job. He said that anyone could play the part under all that makeup. And it was also said that he was too conceited to take the job. He didn't want a part where he would not be recognized and would not have any lines to speak.

So Karloff was offered the job. He turned in a fine performance as a monster who suffered because of the scientific work of another person. Twelve years later, Lugosi got another chance. He played the monster in *Frankenstein Meets the Wolf Man.*

Even before he went in front of the cameras, Karloff was probably worn out. His makeup took three hours to put on, every day. First of all, he had struts in his trousers to make his legs stiff. He

Here is the great job of makeup: Karloff as the monster in *Frankenstein.* (Universal, 1931)

wore a steel spine, so he could not bend over very well. And he wore huge boots—the heavy kind that were used by men who spread asphalt on roads in those days. His whole costume weighed forty-eight pounds. That doesn't even include the makeup for his face.

After he was prepared, he had to put in a full

day on the set. And it was August at the time. Imagine trying to act in that outfit under a hot Los Angeles sun. This may have helped him perform better as a suffering monster. He probably really was suffering.

Here is the laboratory set from *Frankenstein.* Dr. Frankenstein, in the light coat, is played by Colin Clive. Dwight Frye is his assistant. (Universal, 1931)

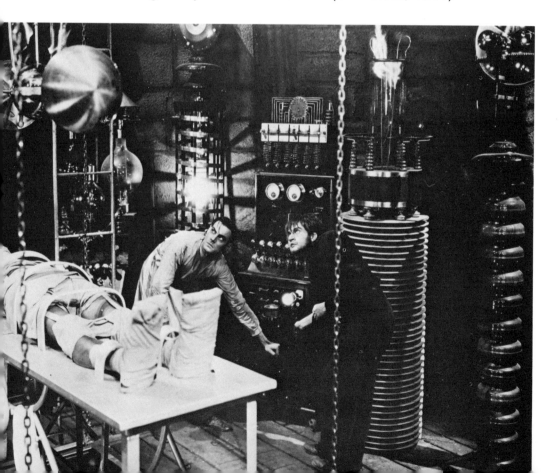

Several other people besides Karloff and Lugosi played the Frankenstein monster. Glenn Strange was one. And here is a sort of coincidence. Strange had been the bad guy in many cowboy films before he was hired to play the monster. Years later he was a regular in the *Gunsmoke* television series. Until his death in the early 1970s, he was the bartender in the Long Branch Saloon. And who was he acting with? James Arness, as Matt Dillon. The coincidence is that Arness, early in his career, also played a monster. He was the star of *The Thing*.

THE GREATEST MOON-MADE MONSTER
The Wolf Man

The best werewolf film was made in 1941. It is called *The Wolf Man,* and stars Lon Chaney, Jr. Chaney was the son of Lon Chaney, Sr., of course. Chaney, Sr., was the most outstanding actor in horror films during the silent movie days.

The story takes place in Transylvania, as you might guess. Lawrence Talbot, played by Chaney, is a happy college student. On a vacation, he goes for a walk one night. Then he makes his mistake. He breaks up a fight between a young woman and a werewolf. During the scuffle the werewolf bites him. Talbot is infected and becomes a werewolf himself.

Talbot starts having what he thinks are dreams. In the dreams he kills people. To get help, he goes to an old Gypsy woman. She tells him that it was her son who bit him. She also tells him that his dreams were real. He is a werewolf and he *has*

Lon Chaney, Jr., as the Wolf Man. What a makeup job!
(Universal, 1941)

been killing people. He will not be able to stop until he is killed by a silver bullet or some other silver object.

Talbot goes on killing. He finds his victims by looking in the palms of their hands. There he sees a mysterious five-pointed figure called a pentagram. He dreads the nights of the full moon. It is then that he turns into a werewolf and does his dirty work.

Finally, Talbot is killed by his own father. His father clubs him to death with a silver-headed cane.

The film was an instant success. Chaney was very good as Talbot. And he had help from two other fine horror movie actors. Bela Lugosi played the Gypsy woman's son. And Claude Rains, who had been the star of *The Invisible Man,* played Talbot's father.

But the next time you see the picture, you might want to be a little picky. It could have been more accurate. Let's take a look at the werewolf legend.

For centuries, all over the world, people have believed in werewolves. But almost all the old stories say that a werewolf brings his problem on himself. He has to want to become a werewolf. This is done by magic. The stories say that you can't become a werewolf by being bitten by one.

They say that the only thing that you become if a werewolf attacks you is a dinner for the werewolf.

Also, a man who turns into a werewolf does not go around in what looks like a garage mechanic's uniform, walking on his hind legs. He actually turns into a wolf. A large hungry wolf.

Most of the stories say that a silver object will kill a werewolf. Especially a silver bullet. And the bullet is more effective if it is blessed by a priest. But people also believed that you didn't have to kill a werewolf. It could be cured. You could call it by its human name while it was in the form of a wolf, for example. Or take blood from its head while it was in the wolf form.

And, if the werewolf wanted to be a human forever it was thought that all it had to do was to go without meat for one hundred years. But that is quite an order.

Finally, the pentagram is a witch symbol, and has nothing to do with werewolves.

The Wolf Man was not the first werewolf picture. *The Werewolf* was made in 1913 in the United States. It was a silent picture, of course, and was not about a wolf man at all. It was about a wolf woman and was based on an old Navajo Indian legend.

Henry Hull in his laboratory in *The Werewolf of London.*
Compare his makeup with Chaney's. (Universal, 1935)

The first talking wolf man appeared in 1935 in a film called *The Werewolf of London.* It stars Henry Hull as a botanist who has been bitten by a werewolf. There's that old mistake again.

The Werewolf of London was not a great success. But *The Wolf Man* was. And one of the reasons for this was the great job of makeup on Lon Chaney, Jr. It was created by Jack Pierce, the same makeup man who had designed Karloff's monster face.

In the movie, Chaney was turned into a werewolf right on the screen. To do this, they applied the makeup in front of the camera. A few frames

Michael Landon in *I Was a Teenage Werewolf*. (American
International, 1957)

of film of Chaney without his makeup were exposed. Then the camera was stopped. Some hair was glued to Chaney's face and hands. Again the camera was started for a few frames and stopped. A few more hairs were glued on, and so on. It took five hours of filming for Chaney to go through the change from Talbot to wolf.

There were many sequels to *The Wolf Man.* Two of them were quite unusual.

The most complicated was *Abbott and Costello Meet Frankenstein.* Yes, the wolf man was in that. He saved Costello's life. An evil scientist wanted to put the little man's brain in his homemade monster, but the wolf man grabbed the villain and leaped into the sea.

Then there was *I Was a Teenage Werewolf.* This one starred Michael Landon before he became a star on the *Bonanza* and *Little House on the Prairie* TV series. A Hollywood producer read that seven out of every ten moviegoers were between twelve and twenty-five years old. So he made a movie about a young wolf man. It was a success. The producer spent $150,000 on the movie and got back $2,300,000.

The Mummy

The Mummy, starring Boris Karloff, was made in 1932. Karloff played an ancient Egyptian priest named Im-ho-tep. Im-ho-tep falls in love with a princess. The princess dies, but the priest has a plan. He can bring her back to life. All he has to do is to steal the Scroll of Thoth, a book of magic, from the temple.

But he gets caught. And the other priests and the pharaoh wrap him up as a mummy and bury him alive. Without a funeral service. So he spends the next few centuries guarding his sweetheart's mummy.

Then the picture switches to the present century. The mummy of the princess is discovered by scientists. One of them accidentally reads from the Scroll of Thoth. This brings Im-ho-tep back to life, and he takes on the identity of Ardath Bey. He is

Boris Karloff as the sleeping Im-ho-tep in *The Mummy.*
(Universal, 1932)

pretending to be an Egyptian scholar. But he is
still guarding his princess.

The mummy of the princess is taken to the
Cairo Museum. Ardath Bey has stolen the Scroll of
Thoth and tries again to bring the girl back to life.
He is discovered by the scientists and fails.

Bey then finds a beautiful young woman named Helen. He thinks she is the princess brought back to life. But when he tries to explain this to her, she prays to the goddess Isis for help. The goddess turns Bey to dust.

Karloff played both the priest and Ardath Bey in the film. Several other people played the mummy in other films. Lon Chaney, Jr., was one of them. But no one was as good as Karloff. He was a fine actor. And his thin body and gleaming eyes helped to frighten the audience.

The idea for this film came from the ancient Egyptian religion. The Egyptians once believed that a dead person could not have a happy afterlife without his body. So they preserved the dead body as best they could. They developed mummification to a high degree.

The time came when they could produce beautiful mummies. Some of them had artificial eyes. Most mummies were packed inside to make them look more lifelike. But the Egyptians did not believe that a mummy could come back to life here on earth. The mummy was made for the afterworld. Just another example of Hollywood's twisting a legend to make a scary picture.

THE GREATEST INSECT MONSTER
The Fly

The Fly is a film about a scientist who goes wrong. It is so entertaining because it is rather unusual. The scientist is not evil or mad. He loves his family. And he dies rather than be a burden to the human race.

He makes a machine that can transport things from one place to another. Not like a railroad train or an airplane. This machine can make an object disappear from one place, and reappear someplace else, without being seen to move.

The scientist has two glass cases, one on each side of his laboratory. When he turns on the machine, an object disappears from one case, and then reappears in the other.

Naturally he tries to send his own body from one case to the other. But he doesn't know that there is a housefly in the case he thinks is empty. When the experiment is over, he finds a horrible

David Hedison, as the Fly, in his laboratory. (Twentieth Century–Fox, 1958)

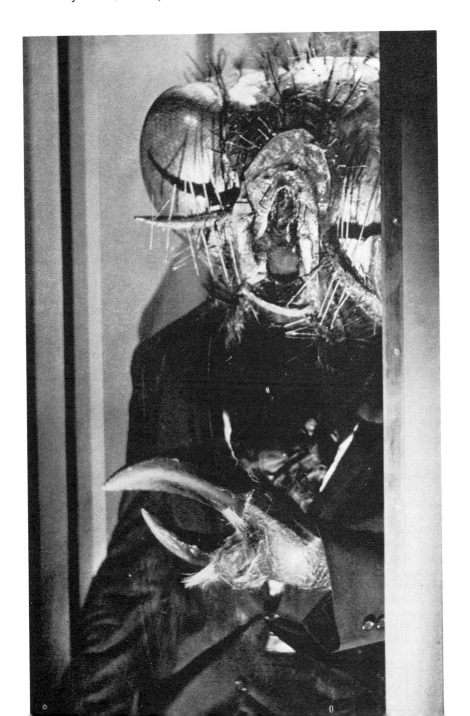

thing has happened. He has ended up with a fly's head and arm on his body. And the fly has ended up with the scientist's head and arm on its body.

The fly with the human head escapes. And after a time the scientist realizes he can never turn back into his own form again.

So he makes a decision. The world must not know about his experiment. He has his wife help him to commit suicide by squashing the horrible head in a press. The fly with the human head later is found in a web. But it ends up as a spider's dinner.

Maybe you want to ask a question or two. How did the scientist keep his own brain inside the fly's head? And if the fly with the human head had a fly's brain inside, how was it able to speak?

THE GREATEST VAMPIRE MONSTER

Dracula

The film *Dracula* was made in the same year as *Frankenstein*. In the opening scene a young man is riding in a carriage. He is on his way to Castle Dracula. The castle is a spooky place filled with cobwebs. There are huge empty staircases and cold fireplaces.

Soon after the young man arrives, he meets Count Dracula, the castle's owner. Dracula is tall, white-faced, and smiling. He is dressed in a tail-coat, and obviously is enjoying himself. Eventually, the young man is turned into a vampire. He ends up eating flies and laughing to himself.

Dracula, apparently running out of victims, leaves Transylvania and goes to England on a ship. In London he is invited to parties and treated like a nobleman. However, he turns a young woman named Lucy into a vampire. He does this by biting her in the neck, of course. At the end of the film,

Who wouldn't be frightened to meet Lugosi in *Dracula?* Look at those eyes. And look at those cobwebs. (Universal, 1931)

Dracula is defeated by Dr. Van Helsing, a vampire expert.

The movie *Dracula* was taken from a book of the same name. It was written by Bram Stoker and published in 1897. But the legends of vampires are ancient. The early Greeks believed in blood-sucking monsters called empusas and striges and lamias. The modern version of the vampire is an eastern European invention.

Lugosi as Dracula, and as one of his victims, Helen Chandler. (Universal, 1931)

According to eastern Europeans, the vampire is thin and looks like a corpse. It has thick red lips and sharp pointed teeth. Its skin is white and cold. And its fingernails are long. This is the most popular description.

The legends say that a vampire can exist forever. It cannot be killed, because it is already dead. But it can be put out of action. A silver bullet is supposed to work. Or a stake driven through the heart.

The vampire is supposed to remain in its coffin from dawn until nightfall. It cannot stand daylight. It also cannot throw a shadow. It has no reflection in a mirror. But it can change into an animal or even into a patch of fog. It can be driven away with a crucifix or garlic.

Most of the old stories tell how to become a vampire. Just let a vampire bite you. Some tales say that once is not enough. You have to be bitten for several nights straight.

These were the legends that Stoker borrowed for his book.

The first choice to play the Count in the film was Lon Chaney, Sr. But he died before shooting began. So Bela Lugosi was chosen. He had been in

That coffin was a vampire's bed in *Dracula.* (Universal, 1931)

a play, *Dracula,* so he knew the vampire's character.

Lugosi was great. He seemed completely evil. The settings, especially Castle Dracula, were terrifying, too.

Dracula was not the first vampire picture. There was a French film, *The Devil's Castle,* made in 1896. A German film, *Nosferatu,* was made in 1922. Then, in 1927, Lon Chaney, Sr., appeared in *London After Midnight.*

He played a vampire with a kind of insane look. He had wide, staring eyes with circles around

Lon Chaney, Sr., as a vampire in *London After Midnight*.
(Metro-Goldwyn-Mayer, 1927)

them. His teeth seemed to be filed to sharp points.
His hair was a mess.

Chaney suffered with this makeup. He used thin
wires to make his eyes bulge. He wore a set of false
animal teeth. The teeth hurt him so much that he
could not wear them for more than a few minutes.

Lon Chaney, Jr., as a vampire in *Son of Dracula.* (Universal, 1943)

Then came Lugosi. And afterward, such vampires as John Carradine. And Lon Chaney, Jr. What a coincidence. The son played the role long after the father had died. Chaney, Jr., did not play Dracula. He played another vampire character named Alucard. But just spell that backward.

THE GREATEST MONSTER SEQUEL

The Bride of Frankenstein

Monster movies often make a lot of money. The producers of the Karloff *Frankenstein* spent $750,000 on it. They eventually got back more than $13,000,000. That's a lot of profit. No wonder they wanted to make another monster picture about Frankenstein.

Let's talk a little about names. In Mary Shelley's book, *Frankenstein,* the doctor's first name was Victor. There is nothing wrong with that. Who knows why the movie people changed it to Henry? Or why they never gave the monster a name in the film. In the book, he was called Adam. This was probably because he was the first artificial man. And Adam was the first real man.

Maybe the fact that he had no name caused the confusion. You probably know many people who think that the monster's name was Frankenstein. But that was the doctor's name.

Hollywood did not help the problem when it came out with *The Bride of Frankenstein* in 1935. It wasn't a picture about Frankenstein's bride. It was a picture about Frankenstein's monster's bride.

The first meeting of the two monsters in *The Bride of Frankenstein.* Left to right: Colin Clive, Elsa Lanchester, Boris Karloff, Ernest Thesiger. (Universal, 1935)

And it was a good one. It starred Karloff as the monster. Colin Clive, the Dr. Frankenstein of the other picture, played the part again. And Elsa Lanchester was the bride. There are some people who think that *The Bride of Frankenstein* was even better than *Frankenstein*.

The monster is in love. But the Bride of Frankenstein is terrified. (Universal, 1935)

In the sequel, the monster is more like the monster in the original book. He does not hate. He wants company. So Dr. Frankenstein decides to build a woman monster to be his companion.

When he finally brings the woman to life, a horrible thing happens. She takes one look at the monster and will have nothing to do with him.

The woman is screaming with fright. But the monster reaches out to pat her hand. He seems to be trying to show her that he needs someone to love. But it doesn't work.

Shedding a tear, the monster forces Dr. and Mrs. Frankenstein to leave the laboratory. When they have gone, he blows up the building. Both monsters are destroyed. Or so it seems. But you know that the Frankenstein monster will be back in many more pictures.

THE GREATEST SELF-MADE MONSTER

Mr. Hyde

You may have seen a horror film that gave you a bad dream. But there is a case of a bad dream giving someone a movie.

It didn't really happen exactly that way. But the English author Robert Louis Stevenson said that he got a story idea from a dream. The story turned out to be *The Strange Case of Dr. Jekyll and Mr. Hyde,* written in 1886.

Dr. Jekyll is a lovable man. But he is experimenting in his laboratory too much. He makes a liquid that will turn him into Mr. Hyde. Hyde is a truly evil man. Jekyll also invents a liquid that will turn him back to normal.

He keeps experimenting. He changes into Mr. Hyde and back into Dr. Jekyll many times. But finally he learns that he has committed a crime while he was Mr. Hyde. He is now a murderer.

Naturally, Jekyll decides to stop taking the liquid. But it is too late. He finds that he turns into the evil Mr. Hyde without taking the drug. He has to take double doses to turn back into Dr. Jekyll. Finally, he runs out of one of the chemicals and cannot change back. But there is still a little of the Dr. Jekyll conscience left. He knows that he will eventually remain a total monster. So he commits suicide.

Many movies have been based on this story. They have been made in Italy, France, England, and the United States. Even Abbott and Costello once met Dr. Jekyll and Mr. Hyde. The three outstanding films were American.

The strange part is that you probably will never see the best two. One was a silent picture. The other just is not shown often. However, they deserve mention.

The silent *Dr. Jekyll and Mr. Hyde* was made in 1920, starring John Barrymore. Barrymore was one of the outstanding stage actors of the day. And he played the role to perfection. Both roles, that is.

His changing scenes were amazing. The camera focused on him as Dr. Jekyll, full face. Slowly he drank the drug. Then he fell from his chair to the floor. Now he was out of range of the camera.

The camera was stopped. Barrymore put on his

John Barrymore, as
the evil Mr. Hyde.
(Paramount, 1920)

ugly makeup. The camera was started again.
When the actor got up he was Mr. Hyde.

The first American talking *Dr. Jekyll and Mr.
Hyde* was made in 1932. It starred Fredric March.
So far he is the only actor ever to receive an Academy Award Oscar for appearing in a monster
movie.

It was a great performance. March played Hyde
the way Karloff had played Frankenstein's monster. It was almost as if he was a pathetic beast.
The camera, by the way, looked Jekyll right in the
face as he was changing. No one ever told the secret of how that was done.

The third American *Dr. Jekyll and Mr. Hyde,* the

Dr. Jekyll and Mr. Hyde. A before-and-after photograph
of Fredric March. (Paramount, 1932)

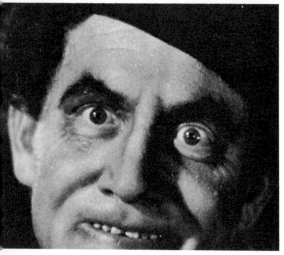

Three shots of Spencer Tracy changing from Dr. Jekyll to Mr. Hyde. Notice the small amount of makeup he used. (Metro-Goldwyn-Mayer, 1941)

one that you may have seen, is the 1941 film with Spencer Tracy. It also starred Ingrid Bergman and Lana Turner. Tracy was good. He was good enough to play Hyde without much makeup. Fake eyebrows and eye shadow were about all that he used. But the script was not the best. And some dream sequences slowed down the film.

Maybe there will be another, and better, version. Perhaps in color.

THE GREATEST NOTHING MONSTER
The Invisible Man

The Invisible Man is based on a book by H. G. Wells. Wells also wrote such wonderful books as *The War of the Worlds* and *The First Men in the Moon.* Both of these have been made into movies, too.

The story of the picture is simple. A mysterious stranger turns up in a small English village. His head is covered with bandages. He is wearing gloves and dark glasses. In fact, no part of his body can be seen.

His name is Dr. Griffen, and he is a chemist. Griffen has discovered a formula that can change his body. It makes him invisible. But there is a problem. The chemicals have also made him crazy.

He wants to rule the world. And he starts by making trains go off the tracks. He also robs banks and murders people. At the end of the picture he is caught and shot. As he dies, he becomes visible again.

The chemist was played by Claude Rains. He

Claude Rains behind his bandages in *The Invisible Man.*
Gloria Stuart is with him. (Universal, 1933)

was the man who played the father in *The Wolf
Man.* And he got the part in a way that may sound
familiar to you. Remember when Karloff played
the Frankenstein monster because Lugosi didn't

want the job? Lugosi said that he didn't want a role where he would not be recognized on the screen. Now it was Karloff's turn. He didn't want a part where he would be invisible until the end of the picture. So Karloff was helpful to Rains in the same way Lugosi had been helpful to Karloff. By accident, of course.

The filmmakers did a wonderful job of trick photography in this picture. One of the best scenes comes when the chemist unwinds his bandages. As he is taking them off, you see that there is nothing under them. You can look right through his head.

They used two techniques for this. The first was double exposure. All this means is that the film was exposed twice. The second was a masked negative. This means that a part of the image was blacked out on the film. On one exposure, against a black background, the actor's head was blotted out by treating the film. Then, when this was combined with the other exposure of the background, the scenery showed through. Right where the head was supposed to be.

The trick worked. And it was used again in 1940, when Vincent Price made *The Invisible Man Returns*.

Dr. Moreau's Creatures

H. G. Wells wrote another fine book called *The Island of Dr. Moreau*. This was made into the movie *The Island of Lost Souls*.

The film is about a mad scientist who lives on an island. He is trying to turn animals into humans. He does his experiments by performing painful operations on the animals.

His biggest success is a girl named Lola. She was once a panther. And at times she still acts more like a cat than a woman.

All the while, the doctor has taught his animal people to be gentle. They don't even realize that they can be violent. They think that only the doctor has the power to be cruel.

Then Moreau orders one of his ape men to commit a murder. So the animals learn that they can revolt against the scientist. They take him to his own operating room and torture him in the same way he had tortured them. At the end, there is a fire and everything burns up.

Probably the most interesting thing about the picture is the acting. Bela Lugosi played the part

Charles Laughton whipping his monsters in *The Island of Lost Souls*. The one in the center with the most hair is Bela Lugosi. (Paramount, 1933)

of the leader of the animal people. And the part of Dr. Moreau was played by Charles Laughton.

Laughton was a fine English actor. At the time of the film he was almost unknown in this country. Later, he made quite a hit in the original movie of *Mutiny on the Bounty*, with Clark Gable. However, the most interesting thing of all is that he was married to Elsa Lanchester. That's right. She was the Bride of Frankenstein.

THE GREATEST COPYCAT MONSTERS

All through the 1930s and the 1940s, the most successful horror movie studio was Universal. Universal put out *Frankenstein, Dracula, The Mummy, The Wolf Man,* and many, many more. Then, in the 1950s, an English company, Hammer, took over.

Hammer took the *Frankenstein* story and turned it into *The Curse of Frankenstein.* The film starred Peter Cushing as Frankenstein and Christopher Lee as the monster. Lee did not use the same makeup as Karloff had. Universal Studios still owned the rights to that.

Hammer made so much money with this film that they made *The Revenge of Frankenstein* the very next year. Then they redid *Dracula.* But they called it *Horror of Dracula.* Lee was the vampire and Cushing was Dr. Van Helsing, the man who defeats him.

Then came *The Mummy,* with the same two ac-

Christopher Lee in *The Curse of Frankenstein.* Compare his monster makeup with Karloff's. Which is more frightening? (Hammer, 1957)

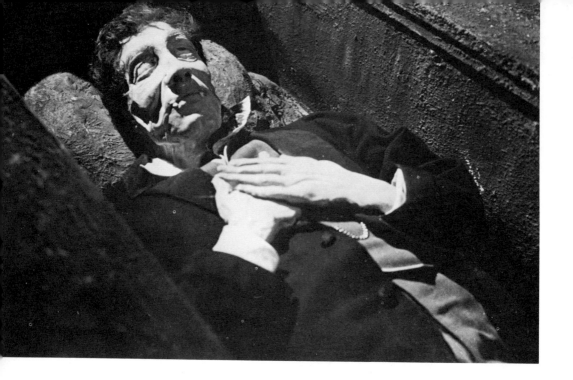

One of the vampire gang in *Horror of Dracula*. He is played by John Van Eyssen. (Hammer, 1958)

tors. And they even borrowed from *The Wolf Man* and came out with *The Curse of the Werewolf*. This starred the fine actor Oliver Reed. Hammer also made *The Two Faces of Dr. Jekyll*. They ended up making sequels to their own movies, such as *The Evil of Frankenstein*, *The Curse of the Mummy's Tomb*, and *Dracula, Prince of Darkness*. All of them were interesting copies of earlier movies.

The British version of *The Mummy.* Christopher Lee is the mummy and Peter Cushing is trying to fight him off. (Hammer, 1959)

Oliver Reed carries off a victim in *The Curse of the Werewolf.* Compare his makeup with Lon Chaney, Jr.'s. (Hammer, 1961)

THE GREATEST MONSTER ACTORS

As far as anyone knows, the first monster movies were made in France in the 1890s. But it took thirty years for them to become popular in the United States. Then Lon Chaney, Sr., became famous. In the 1920s, he was the most noted monster actor of them all.

Chaney played in silent movies. But it did not make any difference. Chaney was a great actor. He could show you how he felt without making a sound. And he was a master of makeup. Very few actors put on their own makeup. Chaney invented his.

In 1930, shortly after the first talking picture was made, Chaney died. His place in horror movies was taken by two men. One of them was the English-born Boris Karloff. The other was the Hungarian-born Bela Lugosi.

Karloff was a fine actor. He was also good

The first master of horror. Lon Chaney, Sr., as the Phantom of the Opera. (Universal, 1925)

They look pleasant without their make-up, don't they? Bela Lugosi, left, and Boris Karloff.

enough to play horror parts that did not require much makeup. And good enough to make people feel sympathy for a monster, too.

Lugosi seemed to be a better actor without makeup. When he played Dracula, everyone shivered. But when he played really ugly monsters, he was not as good. You might even have thought that he was embarrassed.

Then along came Lon Chaney, Jr. He could act. You know that if you have seen some of his non-monster movies. But he was usually given pretty awful roles to play. Either the story was ridiculous or the part was not good. But he carried on his father's work.

The days of these four men are over. But three others have come along to take their place. The first is Peter Cushing. Cushing can play mad scientists like Frankenstein. He can play normal scientists like Dr. Van Helsing. He can play brilliant scientists like Sherlock Holmes. And he can do them all well.

Christopher Lee is great as a monster. He has been a vampire, a mummy, the Frankenstein monster, and many other creepy characters.

Finally, there is Vincent Price. He can play a

In *Frankenstein Meets the Wolf Man,* Bela Lugosi was the monster. Here Lon Chaney, Jr., suspects that he will soon turn into a werewolf. (Universal, 1943)

Here is the laboratory in *The Curse of Frankenstein.* Frankenstein (Peter Cushing) looks at his monster (Christopher Lee) while Robert Urquhart stands by. (Hammer, 1957)

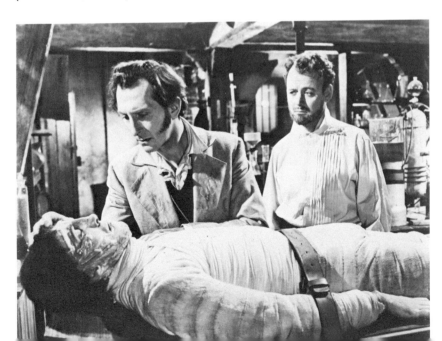

mad scientist, a crippled monster, or a great detective. And he makes his job look easy. This is because he has a sense of humor. He seems to be having a good time in his films.

There have been so many monster movies it might seem that we have run out of monsters. But there may be a new one. The machine monster.

Jolly Vincent Price in *The Pit and the Pendulum.* (American International, 1961)

You can't kill a monster machine. All you can do is unplug it.

We met the monster machine in *2001: A Space Odyssey*. It was a computer on board a space ship. Its name was Hal.

Hal had a mind of his own. He tried to kill the space travelers. What was he but the man-made monster of many horror films?

What will they think up next?

MORE ABOUT SOME OF THE FILMS

ABBOTT AND COSTELLO MEET FRANKENSTEIN (Universal, 1948).

Director: Charles Barton.

With Bud Abbott, Lou Costello, Lon Chaney, Jr., Bela Lugosi, Glenn Strange.

BEAST OF HOLLOW MOUNTAIN, THE (United Artists, Peliculas Rodriguez, 1956).

Director: Edward Nassour, Ismael Rodriguez.

With Guy Madison, Patricia Medina.

BRIDE OF FRANKENSTEIN, THE (Universal, 1935).

Director: James Whale.

With Boris Karloff, Colin Clive, Elsa Lanchester, Ernest Thesiger, Dwight Frye, Una O'Conner, Mary Gordon, Walter Brennan, John Carradine.

CREATURE FROM THE BLACK LAGOON, THE (Universal, 1954).

Director: Jack Arnold.

With Richard Carlson, Julia Adams, Richard Denning, Ricou Browning, Whit Bissell.

CURSE OF FRANKENSTEIN, THE (Hammer, 1957).
> *Director:* Terence Fisher.
> *With* Peter Cushing, Christopher Lee, Hazel Court.

CURSE OF THE MUMMY'S TOMB, THE (Hammer-Swallow, 1964).
> *Director:* Michael Carreras.
> *With* Ronald Howard, Terence Morgan, Fred Clark.

CURSE OF THE WEREWOLF, THE (Hammer, 1961).
> *Director:* Terence Fisher.
> *With* Oliver Reed, Clifford Evans, Yvonne Romain.

DEVIL'S CASTLE, THE (Robert-Houdin, 1896).
> *Director:* George Méliès.

DR. JEKYLL AND MR. HYDE (Paramount, 1920).
> *Director:* John S. Robertson.
> *With* John Barrymore, Nita Naldi, Louis Wolheim.

DR. JEKYLL AND MR. HYDE (Paramount, 1932).
> *Director:* Rouben Mamoulian.
> *With* Fredric March, Miriam Hopkins, Rose Hobart.

DR. JEKYLL AND MR. HYDE (MGM, 1941).
> *Director:* Victor Fleming.
> *With* Spencer Tracy, Ingrid Bergman, Lana Turner, Ian Hunter, Donald Crisp, Barton MacLane, C. Aubrey Smith.

DRACULA (Universal, 1931).
> *Director:* Tod Browning.
> *With* Bela Lugosi, Helen Chandler, Dwight Frye.

DRACULA, PRINCE OF DARKNESS (Hammer, 1965).
> *Director:* Terence Fisher.
> *With* Christopher Lee, Barbara Shelley.

EVIL OF FRANKENSTEIN, THE (Hammer, 1964).
  Director: Freddie Francis.
  With Peter Cushing.
FLY, THE (Twentieth Century–Fox, 1958).
  Director: Kurt Neumann.
  With David Hedison, Patricia Owens, Vincent Price, Herbert Marshall.
FRANKENSTEIN (Universal, 1931).
  Director: James Whale.
  With Boris Karloff, Colin Clive, Mae Clark, John Boles, Dwight Frye.
FRANKENSTEIN MEETS THE WOLF MAN (Universal, 1943).
  Director: Roy William Neill.
  With Ilona Massey, Patrick Knowles, Lon Chaney, Jr., Lionel Atwill, Bela Lugosi, Maria Ouspenskaya, Dwight Frye.
GODZILLA, KING OF THE MONSTERS (Toho, 1955).
  Director: Inoshiro Honda.
  With Raymond Burr.
HORROR OF DRACULA (Hammer, 1958).
  Director: Terence Fisher.
  With Christopher Lee, Peter Cushing.
I WAS A TEENAGE WEREWOLF (American International, 1957).
  Director: Gene Fowler, Jr.
  With Michael Landon, Whit Bissell, Guy Williams.

INVISIBLE MAN, THE (Universal, 1933).
 Director: James Whale.
 With Claude Rains, Gloria Stuart.
INVISIBLE MAN RETURNS, THE (Universal, 1940).
 Director: Joe May.
 With Sir Cedric Hardwicke, Vincent Price, Alan Napier.
ISLAND OF LOST SOULS (Paramount, 1933).
 Director: Erle C. Kenton.
 With Charles Laughton, Bela Lugosi, Richard Arlen, Leila Hyams.
KING KONG (RKO, 1933).
 Director: Merian C. Cooper, Ernest B. Schoedsack.
 With Fay Wray, Robert Armstrong, Bruce Cabot.
LIFE WITHOUT SOUL (Ocean Film Corporation, 1915).
 Director: Joseph W. Smiley.
 With Percy Darrell Standing.
LONDON AFTER MIDNIGHT (MGM, 1927).
 Director: Tod Browning.
 With Lon Chaney, Sr., Conrad Nagel.
MIGHTY JOE YOUNG (RKO, 1949).
 Director: Ernest B. Schoedsack.
 With Terry Moore, Robert Armstrong.
MUMMY, THE (Universal, 1932).
 Director: Karl Freund.
 With Boris Karloff, Zita Johann, David Manners, Bramwell Fletcher.

MUMMY, THE (Hammer, 1959).

Director: Terence Fisher.

With Peter Cushing, Christopher Lee.

NOSFERATU (Prana, 1922).

Director: F. W. Murnau.

With Max Schreck.

PHANTOM OF THE OPERA, THE (Universal, 1925).

Director: Rupert Julian.

With Lon Chaney, Sr.

PIT AND THE PENDULUM, THE (American-International, 1961).

Director: Roger Corman.

With Vincent Price, John Kerr, Barbara Steele.

REVENGE OF FRANKENSTEIN, THE (Hammer, 1958).

Director: Terence Fisher.

With Peter Cushing.

SON OF DRACULA (Universal, 1943).

Director: Robert Siodmak.

With Lon Chaney, Jr., Robert Paige, Louise Allbritton.

SON OF KONG (RKO, 1933).

Director: Ernest B. Schoedsack.

With Robert Armstrong, Helen Mack.

THING, THE (RKO, 1951).

Director: Howard Hawks.

With Margaret Sheridan, Kenneth Tobey, James Arness.

TWO FACES OF DR. JEKYLL, THE (Hammer, 1960).

Director: Terence Fisher.

With Christopher Lee.

VAMPIRO, EL (Abel Salazar/Cinematográfica A.B.S.A., 1959).

Director: Fernando Méndez.

With Germán Robles, Adriana Welter.

WEREWOLF, THE (Bison, 1913).

Director: Henry McRae.

WEREWOLF OF LONDON, THE (Universal, 1935).

Director: Stuart Walker.

With Henry Hull, Warner Oland, Spring Byington.

WOLF MAN, THE (Universal, 1941).

Director: George Waggner.

With Claude Rains, Ralph Bellamy, Warren William, Patrick Knowles, Bela Lugosi, Lon Chaney, Jr., Maria Ouspenskaya.

INDEX

ABOUT THE AUTHOR

Thomas G. Aylesworth was born in Valparaiso, Indiana, and received his A.B. and M.S. degrees from Indiana University and his Ph.D. from The Ohio State University. He has been a high school teacher, a college professor, and a senior editor of a junior high school weekly science newspaper. He is currently a senior editor at a major New York publishing house. He has written books for young readers on science, the occult, and movies. He lives in Stamford, Connecticut, with his wife and their two children.